TABLE DES MATIÈRES

1. INTRODUCTION

In this book, we want to ensure that learning Dart is as efficient and straightforward as possible for our readers. To achieve this, we have designed all the examples and exercises to be easily performed using DartPad https://dartpad.dev/, an online code editor for Dart development.

Using DartPad offers several advantages. First, it eliminates the need for setting up a local development environment, saving you valuable time and potential configuration headaches. With DartPad, you can focus on learning and experimenting with Dart code immediately, without any installation or setup processes.

Furthermore, DartPad provides an interactive coding environment that allows you to see the results of your code in real-time. As you type your Dart code, DartPad dynamically executes it and displays the output, providing instant feedback on your code's behaviour. This immediate feedback loop facilitates a more hands-on and engaging learning experience.

Additionally, DartPad supports importing external Dart packages, enabling you to leverage the rich ecosystem of existing libraries and frameworks. You can experiment with different packages directly in DartPad, allowing you to explore various functionalities without the need for complex local setups or installations.

We have chosen DartPad as the primary platform for our examples and exercises to streamline your learning experience. By providing a unified environment, we aim to simplify the process of understanding and practicing Dart concepts, making it accessible to readers of all skill levels.

Whether you are a beginner taking your first steps in Dart programming or an experienced developer looking to expand your skill set, DartPad will serve as an invaluable tool throughout your journey. It provides a hassle-free and timesaving approach to coding, allowing you to focus on mastering Dart's core principles and building practical applications.

So, let us dive into the exciting world of Dart programming using DartPad, where you can explore, experiment, and code effortlessly. Get ready to unlock your full potential as a Dart developer and embark on a journey of learning and growth.

1   UNDERSTANDING VARIABLES IN DART

1.1   Introduction to Variables

Variables in Dart are essential for storing and manipulating data. They act as containers that hold different types of values, such as numbers, text, or objects.

1.2   Declaring Variables

In Dart, variables are declared using the `var` keyword followed by a name and an optional type annotation. Let's look at some examples:

var age = 25;

var name = 'Omar';

var temperature = 98.6;

In the above examples, we declared variables `age`, `name`, and `temperature` with inferred types based on the assigned values.

1.3   VARIABLES TYPES

Dart is a statically typed language, meaning variables can have specific types. Here are some common variable types in Dart:

```
int count = 10;
double price = 9.99;
String message = 'Hello, Dart!';
bool isActive = true;
```

In the examples above, we declared variables with explicit types such as `int`, `double`, `String`, and `bool`.

1.4 ASSIGNING VALUES TO VARIABLES

Variables can be assigned values using the assignment operator (`=`). Let's see some examples:

```dart
var x = 5;
x = 10; // Variable x is reassigned a new value
String greeting = 'Hello';
greeting = 'Hi'; // Variable greeting is reassigned a new value
```

In the above code snippets, we assign new values to the variables `x` and `greeting`.

1.5 Working with Constants

Dart also provides constants, which are variables with values that cannot be changed. We can declare constants using the `final` or `const` keywords:

```dart
final int MAX_VALUE = 100;
const double PI = 3.14159;
```

The `final` keyword is used for variables that can be assigned once, while the `const` keyword is used for compile-time constants.

1.6 Variable Scope

Variables have different scopes, determining where they can be accessed within a program. Let's consider an example:

```dart
void myFunction() {
 var message = 'Hello';
 print(message); // Variable message is accessible within the function
}
print(message); // Error: Variable message is not accessible here
```

In the above code snippet, the variable `message` is accessible only within the `myFunction()` function.

1.7 VARIABLE INTERPOLATION

Dart provides string interpolation, allowing you to embed variables within strings. Here's an example:

```dart
var name = 'Leila';
print('Hello, $name!'); // Output: Hello, Leila!
```

In the example, the variable `name` is interpolated within the string using the `$` symbol.

1.8 Variable Operations

Variables can participate in various operations. Let's look at some examples:

```
int a = 5;
int b = 3;
int sum = a + b; // Addition
int difference = a - b; // Subtraction
int product = a * b; // Multiplication
double quotient = a / b; // Division
int remainder = a % b; // Modulo
print(sum); // Output: 8
print(difference); // Output: 2
print(product); // Output: 15
print(quotient); // Output: 1.6666666666666667
print(remainder); // Output: 2
```

The above examples demonstrate various arithmetic operations performed on variables `a` and `b`.

2 FUNCTIONS IN DART

2.1 DECLARING FUNCTIONS

To declare a function in Dart, you need to specify its return type (if any), followed by the function's name and parameter list (if any). The syntax for declaring a function is as follows:

```
returnType functionName(parameter1, parameter2, …) {
  // Function body
  // Code statements
  // Optional return statement
}
```

Here's an example of a simple function that takes two parameters, adds them together, and returns the sum:

```
int addNumbers(int a, int b) {
  int sum = a + b;
  return sum;
}
```

2.2 Invoking Functions

Once you've declared a function, you can invoke or call it by using its name followed by parentheses. If the function expects parameters, you need to provide them within the parentheses. Here's how you can invoke the `addNumbers` function from the previous example:

```
int result = addNumbers(5, 3);

print(result); // Output: 8
```

In the above code snippet, we invoke the `addNumbers` function and pass `5` and `3` as arguments. The returned value, `8`, is stored in the `result` variable, which is then printed to the console.

2.3 DEFAULT PARAMETER VALUES

Dart also supports default parameter values, which allow you to specify default values for function parameters. If an argument is not provided when invoking the function, the default value will be used instead. Here's an example:

```
void greetUser(String name, [String greeting = 'Hello']) {
 print('$greeting, $name!');
}
```

In this case, the `greetUser` function has a default parameter value for the `greeting` parameter, which is set to ''Hello''. If no value is provided for `greeting` when calling the function, it will default to ''Hello''.

```
greetUser('Omar'); // Output: Hello, Omar!
greetUser('Hiba', 'Hi'); // Output: Hi, Hiba!
```

In the above code snippet, the first invocation of `greetUser` only provides the `name` argument, so the default value `"Hello"` is used for `greeting`. The second invocation explicitly provides both `name` and `greeting` arguments.

By understanding the process of declaring and invoking functions in Dart, you can modularize your code and enhance its reusability. Functions are the building blocks of Dart programs, enabling you to encapsulate logic and create efficient, maintainable code.

2.4 EXAMPLES

Here are a few examples of declaring and invoking functions in DartPad:

2.4.1 EXAMPLE 1: SIMPLE ADDITION FUNCTION

```dart
int addNumbers(int a, int b) {
 int sum = a + b;
 return sum;
}
void main() {
 int result = addNumbers(5, 3);
 print(result); // Output: 8
}
```

```
1▾ int addNumbers(int a, int b) {
2    int sum = a + b;
3    return sum;
4  }
5▾ void main() {
6    int result = addNumbers(5, 3);
7    print(result); // Output: 8
8  }
```

Console

▶ Run

8

In this example, we declare a function named `addNumbers` that takes two integer parameters `a` and `b`. The function adds the two numbers together and returns the sum. In the `main` function, we invoke `addNumbers` with arguments `5` and `3`, and the returned value is stored in the `result` variable. Finally, we print the result to the console.

2.4.2 EXAMPLE 2: FUNCTION WITH DEFAULT PARAMETER VALUE

```
void greetUser(String name, [String greeting = 'Hello']) {
 print('$greeting, $name!');
}
void main() {
 greetUser('Leila'); // Output: Hello, Omar!
 greetUser('Adil', 'Hi'); // Output: Hi, Hiba!
}
```

```
1  void greetUser(String name, [String greeting = 'Hello']) {    ▶ Run     Console
2    print('$greeting, $name!');
3  }                                                                        Hello, Leila!
4  void main() {                                                            Hi, Adil!
5    greetUser('Leila'); // Output: Hello, John!
6    greetUser('Adil', 'Hi'); // Output: Hi, Emily!
7  }
```

In this example, we define a function named `greetUser` that takes a mandatory parameter `name` and an optional parameter `greeting` with a default value of ``Hello``. Inside the function, we print a message combining the greeting and the name. In the `main` function, we invoke `greetUser` with only the `name` argument for the first call, resulting in the default greeting being used. For the second call, we provide both the `name` and `greeting` arguments to customize the output.

2.4.3 EXAMPLE 3: FUNCTION WITH VOID RETURN TYPE

```
void printMessage(String message) {
 print(message);
}
void main() {
 printMessage('Hello, DartPad!'); // Output: Hello, DartPad!
}
```

```dart
1  void printMessage(String message) {
2    print(message);
3  }
4  void main() {
5    printMessage('Hello, DartPad!'); // Output: Hello, DartPad!
6  }
```

Run

Console

Hello, DartPad!

In this example, we declare a function named `printMessage` that takes a string parameter `message` and simply prints it to the console. The function has a return type of `void`, indicating that it does not return a value. In the `main` function, we invoke `printMessage` with the argument `'Hello, DartPad!'`, resulting in the message being printed to the console.

3 CONTROL FLOW STATEMENTS

Control flow statements allow you to control the execution flow of your program. They determine which code blocks should be executed based on certain conditions or repeat a set of instructions multiple times. Here are the two main types of control flow statements: conditionals and loops.

3.1 CONDITIONALS

Conditionals allow you to execute specific blocks of code based on certain conditions. Dart provides the following conditional statements:

if statement: The `if` statement executes a block of code if a given condition is true. Optionally, you can include an `else` statement to provide an alternative block of code to execute if the condition is false.

```
if (condition) {
  // code to execute if the condition is true
} else {
  // code to execute if the condition is false
}
```

else if statement: You can extend the `if` statement with additional conditions using the `else if` statement.

```
if (condition1) {
// code to execute if condition1 is true
} else if (condition2) {
// code to execute if condition2 is true
} else {
// code to execute if both conditions are false
}
```

- switch statement: The `switch` statement allows you to choose from multiple code blocks based on the value of an expression. It's useful when you have a large number of possible cases.

```
switch (expression) {
case value1:
// code to execute if expression matches value1
break;
case value2:
// code to execute if expression matches value2
break;
// more cases…
default:
// code to execute if no case matches
}
```

3.2 LOOPS

Loops allow you to repeat a block of code multiple times until a certain condition is met. Dart provides several types of loops:

for loop: The `for` loop executes a block of code for a specified number of iterations.

```
for (initialization; condition; increment) {
  // code to execute in each iteration
}
```

while loop: The `while` loop executes a block of code repeatedly as long as a given condition remains true.

```
while (condition) {
  // code to execute as long as the condition is true
}
```

do-while loop: The `do-while` loop is like the `while` loop, but it executes the code block at least once before checking the condition.

```
do {
  // code to execute at least once
} while (condition);
```

- **break and continue**: You can use the `break` statement to exit a loop prematurely and the `continue` statement to skip the current iteration and move to the next one.

```
while (condition) {
 if (someCondition) {
break; // exit the loop
}
if (anotherCondition) {
continue; // skip to the next iteration
}
// code to execute in each iteration
}
```

These control flow statements give you the flexibility to make decisions and repeat tasks in your Dart programs based on different conditions. They are fundamental building blocks for creating more complex and dynamic applications.

4 COLLECTIONS: LISTS, SETS, AND MAPS

4.1 LISTS

A List in Dart is an ordered collection of elements. It allows you to store and access data in a specific order. Here is an example:

```dart
void main() {
  List<String> fruits = ['apple', 'banana', 'orange'];
  print(fruits[0]); // Output: apple
  fruits.add('grape');
  fruits.remove('banana');
  print(fruits); // Output: [apple, orange, grape]
}
```

In this example, we declare a List called `fruits` that contains strings. We initialize it with three elements: ``apple``, ``banana``, and ``orange``. We access elements using square brackets and zero-based indexing. We add an element ``grape`` using the `add` method and remove ``banana`` using the `remove` method. Finally, we print the modified list.

4.2 SETS

A Set in Dart is an unordered collection of unique elements. It does not allow duplicate values. Here is an example:

```dart
void main() {
  Set<int> numbers = {1, 2, 3, 4, 5};
  numbers.add(6);
  numbers.remove(3);
  print(numbers); // Output: {1, 2, 4, 5, 6}
}
```

In this example, we declare a Set called `numbers` that contains integers. We initialize it with five elements. We add the element `6` using the `add` method and remove the element `3` using the `remove` method. As Sets are unordered, the order of the elements may vary when printed.

4.3 MAPS

A Map in Dart is an unordered collection of key-value pairs. It allows you to associate values with unique keys. Here's an example:

```dart
void main() {
  Map<String, int> studentMarks = {
    'Leila': 90,
    'Adil': 85,
    'Sara': 92,
  };
  studentMarks['Leila'] = 95;
  studentMarks.remove('Sara');
  print(studentMarks); // Output: {Leila: 95, Adil: 85}
}
```

In this example, we declare a Map called `studentMarks` that maps student names (strings) to their corresponding marks (integers). We initialize it with three key-value pairs. We update the mark for ''Leila`` using square bracket notation, and remove the entry for ''Sara`` using the `remove` method. Finally, we print the modified map.

4.4 EXAMPLES

Here are a few more examples of working with collections in DartPad:

4.4.1 EXAMPLE 1: LIST OPERATIONS

```dart
void main() {
  List<int> numbers = [2, 4, 6, 8, 10];
  // Accessing elements
  int firstNumber = numbers[0];
  int lastNumber = numbers[numbers.length - 1];
  // Modifying elements
  numbers[1] = 12;
  numbers.add(14);
  numbers.remove(6);
  print(numbers); // Output: [2, 12, 8, 10, 14]
  print(firstNumber); // Output: 2
  print(lastNumber); // Output: 10
}
```

```dart
void main() {
  List<int> numbers = [2, 4, 6, 8, 10];
  // Accessing elements
  int firstNumber = numbers[0];
  int lastNumber = numbers[numbers.length - 1];
  // Modifying elements
  numbers[1] = 12;
  numbers.add(14);
  numbers.remove(6);
  print(numbers); // Output: [2, 12, 8, 10, 14]
  print(firstNumber); // Output: 2
  print(lastNumber); // Output: 10
}
```

Console

```
[2, 12, 8, 10, 14]
2
10
```

In this example, we create a List called `numbers` with a few integer elements. We access elements using square brackets and index. We modify elements by assigning new values using the index. We also use the `add` method to append an element and the `remove` method to remove an element from the list. Finally, we print the modified list, as well as the first and last elements.

4.4.2 EXAMPLE 2: SET OPERATIONS

```dart
void main() {
  Set<String> fruits = {'apple', 'banana', 'orange'};
  // Adding elements
  fruits.add('grape');
  fruits.add('banana'); // Duplicate element, not added
  // Removing elements
```

```
fruits.remove('apple');
// Checking membership
bool hasBanana = fruits.contains('banana');
print(fruits); // Output: {banana, orange, grape}
print(hasBanana); // Output: true
}
```

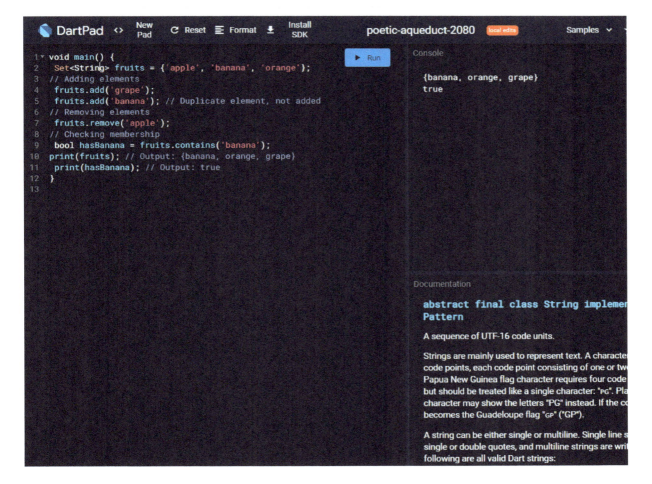

In this example, we declare a Set called `fruits` with some string elements. We use the `add` method to add elements to the set, but since sets do not allow duplicates, the duplicate ``banana`` element is not added. We remove the element ``apple`` using the `remove` method. We check if the set contains the element ``banana`` using the `contains` method. Finally, we print the modified set and the result of the membership check.

4.4.3 EXAMPLE 3: MAP OPERATIONS

```
void main() {
Map<String, int> studentMarks = {
'Leila': 90,
'Adil': 85,
'Sara': 92,
};
// Accessing values
int leilaMarks = studentMarks['Leila']!;
int saraMarks = studentMarks.containsKey('Sara') ? studentMarks['Sara']! : 0;
// Modifying values
studentMarks['Adil'] = 88;
studentMarks.remove('Sara');
print(studentMarks); // Output: {Leila: 90, Adil: 88}
print(leilaMarks); // Output: 90
print(saraMarks); // Output: 0
}
```

```dart
void main() {
  Map<String, int> studentMarks = {
    'Leila': 90,
    'Adil': 85,
    'Sara': 92,
  };
  // Accessing values
  int leilaMarks = studentMarks['Leila']!;
  int saraMarks = studentMarks.containsKey('Sara') ? studentMarks['Sara
  // Modifying values
  studentMarks['Adil'] = 88;
  studentMarks.remove('Sara');
  print(studentMarks); // Output: {Leila: 90, Adil: 88}
  print(leilaMarks); // Output: 90
  print(saraMarks); // Output: 0
}
```

Console
```
{Leila: 90, Adil: 88}
90
92
```

In this example, we define a Map called `studentMarks` that maps student names to their corresponding marks. We access values using square bracket notation and keys. We modify values by assigning new values to the corresponding keys. We use the `remove` method to remove a key-value pair from the map. Finally, we print the modified map, as well as the marks of Leila and Sara.

These examples demonstrate additional operations and functionalities when working with collections in DartPad.

Working with strings and regular expressions is an important aspect of many programming tasks. Here are some examples in DartPad:

5.1.1 EXAMPLE 1: CONCATENATING STRINGS

```dart
void main() {
  String firstName = 'Omar';
  String lastName = 'Hanafi';
  String fullName = firstName + ' ' + lastName;
  print(fullName); // Output: Omar Hanafi
}
```

In this example, we have two strings, `firstName` and `lastName`. We concatenate them using the `+` operator, along with a space, to create the `fullName` string. Finally, we print the concatenated string.

5.1.2 EXAMPLE 2: STRING INTERPOLATION

```dart
void main() {
 String name = 'Leila';
 int age = 25;
String message = 'My name is $name and I am $age years old.';
 print(message); // Output: My name is Leila and I am 25 years old.
 }
```

In this example, we use string interpolation to embed variables within a string using the syntax `$variableName`. The values of the variables `name` and `age` are automatically substituted within the string when it is assigned to `message`. Finally, we print the interpolated string.

5.1.3 EXAMPLE 3: SPLITTING AND JOINING STRINGS

```dart
void main() {
 String sentence = ' Leila is beautiful';
```

```dart
  List<String> words = sentence.split(' ');

  print(words);

String joinedSentence = words.join('-');

  print(joinedSentence);

}
```

```dart
void main() {
  String sentence = 'Leila is beautiful';
  List<String> words = sentence.split(' ');
  print(words); // Output: [The, quick, brown, fox]
  String joinedSentence = words.join('-');
  print(joinedSentence); // Output: The-quick-brown-fox
}
```

Console

[Leila, is, beautiful]
Leila-is-beautiful

In this example, we split a sentence into a list of words using the `split` method, which splits the string at each occurrence of a space character. We then print the resulting list of words. Next, we join the words using the `join` method, specifying the hyphen (`-`) as the separator. Finally, we print the joined sentence.

5.1.4 EXAMPLE 4: REGULAR EXPRESSIONS

```dart
import 'dart:core';
void main() {
  String text = 'Leila and Ahmed are beautiful.';
  RegExp pattern = RegExp(r'Ahmed');
```

```dart
bool hasMatch = pattern.hasMatch(text);
print(hasMatch); // Output: true
Iterable<Match> matches = pattern.allMatches(text);
for (Match match in matches) {
print('Match found at index ${match.start}');
}
}
```

In this example, we use the `RegExp` class from the `dart:core` library to define a regular expression pattern. The pattern `r'Ahmed'` matches the substring ``Ahmed``. We use the `hasMatch` method to check if the pattern has a match in the `text` string. We also use the `allMatches` method to find all occurrences of the pattern in the `text` string and iterate over the matches to print their indices.

These examples provide a glimpse into working with strings and regular expressions in Dart.

```dart
import 'dart:core';
void main() {
  String text = 'Leila and Ahmed are beautiful.';
  RegExp pattern = RegExp(r'Ahmed');
bool hasMatch = pattern.hasMatch(text);
  print(hasMatch); // Output: true
Iterable<Match> matches = pattern.allMatches(text);
  for (Match match in matches) {
  print('Match found at index ${match.start}');
  }
}
```

Console:
```
true
Match found at index 10
```

6 OBJECTS AND CLASSES IN DART

Objects and classes are fundamental concepts in object-oriented programming (OOP). They allow us to model real-world entities, define their properties and behaviours, and interact with them in our programs.

6.1 Objects

— An object is an instance of a class. It represents a specific entity or concept from the real world.

— Objects encapsulate data (properties) and behavior (methods) into a single unit.

— Each object has a state (values of its properties) and can perform actions (invoking methods).

— Objects interact with each other by invoking methods and accessing properties.

6.2 Classes

— A class is a blueprint or template that defines the structure and behavior of objects.

— It serves as a blueprint for creating multiple objects of the same type.

— A class defines the properties (variables) and behaviors (methods) that objects of that class will have.

— Objects of a class share the same structure and behavior defined by the class.

In Dart, classes are defined using the `class` keyword. Here's a basic example:

```dart
class Person {
  String? name;
  int? age;
  void sayHello() {
```

```
      print('Hello, my name is $name!');
    }
  }
```

In the above example, we define a `Person` class with two properties (`name` and `age`) and a method (`sayHello`). We can create objects (instances) of this class and interact with them:

```
void main() {
  var person1 = Person();
  person1.name = 'Omar';
  person1.age = 30;
  var person2 = Person();
  person2.name = 'Leila';
  person2.age = 25;
person1.sayHello(); // Output: Hello, my name is Omar!
  person2.sayHello(); // Output: Hello, my name is Leila!
}
```

```dart
void main() {
  var person1 = Person();
  person1.name = 'Omar';
  person1.age = 30;
  var person2 = Person();
  person2.name = 'Leila';
  person2.age = 25;
  person1.sayHello(); // Output: Hello, my name is Omar!
  person2.sayHello(); // Output: Hello, my name is Leila!
}
class Person {
  String ? name;
  int ? age;
  void sayHello() {
    print('Hello, my name is $name!');
  }
}
```

Console

Hello, my name is Omar!
Hello, my name is Leila!

In the above `main` function, we create two `Person` objects (`person1` and `person2`) and set their properties. We can then invoke the `sayHello` method on each object to display a personalized greeting.

By creating objects from classes, we can organize our code; achieve code reusability, and model complex systems by representing entities and their interactions. Objects and classes are core building blocks in Dart and other object-oriented programming languages.

6.2.1 EXAMPLES IN DART:

Abstraction is a concept in object-oriented programming (OOP) that allows us to represent complex systems by simplifying their models and focusing on the essential aspects. It involves creating abstract classes and interfaces that define common characteristics and behaviors, while hiding the implementation details and unnecessary complexities.

6.2.1.1 EXAMPLE 1: ABSTRACT CLASS

```
abstract class Animal {
 void makeSound(); // Abstract method (no implementation)

 void sleep() {
 print("The animal is sleeping."); // Concrete method with implementation
 }
}
class Dog extends Animal {
 @override
 void makeSound() {
 print("The dog barks.");
 }
}
void main() {
 var dog = Dog();
 dog.makeSound(); // Output: The dog barks.
 dog.sleep(); // Output: The animal is sleeping.
}
```

```
abstract class Animal {
  void makeSound(); // Abstract method (no implementation)

  void sleep() {
    print('The animal is sleeping.'); // Concrete method with implementat
  }
}
class Dog extends Animal {
  @override
  void makeSound() {
    print('The dog barks.');
  }
}
void main() {
  var dog = Dog();
  dog.makeSound(); // Output: The dog barks.
  dog.sleep(); // Output: The animal is sleeping.
}
```

Console

```
The dog barks.
The animal is sleeping.
```

In this example, we have an abstract class called `Animal` with an abstract method `makeSound()` and a concrete method `sleep()`. The `Animal` class defines the common behavior that all animals should have. The `Dog` class extends the `Animal` class and provides an implementation for the `makeSound()` method. We can create an instance of the `Dog` class and invoke both the abstract and concrete methods.

6.2.1.2 EXAMPLE 2: INTERFACE

```
abstract class Flyable {
  void fly();
}
class Bird implements Flyable {
  @override
  void fly() {
```

```dart
    print('The bird is flying.');
  }
}
class Airplane implements Flyable {
  @override
  void fly() {
    print('The airplane is flying.');
  }
}
void main() {
  var bird = Bird();
  bird.fly(); // Output: The bird is flying.

  var airplane = Airplane();
  airplane.fly(); // Output: The airplane is flying.
}
```

```
1  abstract class Flyable {
2    void fly();
3  }
4  class Bird implements Flyable {
5    @override
6    void fly() {
7    print('The bird is flying.');
8    }
9  }
10 class Airplane implements Flyable {
11   @override
12   void fly() {
13   print('The airplane is flying.');
14   }
15 }
16 void main() {
17   var bird = Bird();
18   bird.fly(); // Output: The bird is flying.
19
20   var airplane = Airplane();
21   airplane.fly(); // Output: The airplane is flying.
22 }
23
```

Console

The bird is flying.
The airplane is flying.

Documentation

abstract class Animal

In this example, we define an interface called `Flyable` with a single method `fly()`. The `Bird` class and the `Airplane` class implement the `Flyable` interface by providing their own implementations of the `fly()` method. We can create instances of both the `Bird` and `Airplane` classes and invoke the `fly()` method on each of them.

Through abstraction, we simplify the representation of complex systems by focusing on the essential characteristics and behaviors. Abstract classes and interfaces provide a blueprint for related objects, allowing for code modularity, reusability, and flexibility. By utilizing abstraction, we can create organized and maintainable code structures that can adapt to changing requirements.

6.3 POLYMORPHISM

Polymorphism is a key concept in object-oriented programming (OOP) that enables objects of different classes to be treated as objects of a common superclass or interface. It provides flexibility and adaptability in code design by allowing different objects to respond to the same method calls in their own specific ways.

6.3.1 POLYMORPHISM WITH INHERITANCE:

```
class Shape {
 void draw() {
 print('Drawing a shape.');
 }
}
class Circle extends Shape {
 @override
 void draw() {
 print('Drawing a circle.');
 }
}
class Square extends Shape {
 @override
 void draw() {
 print('Drawing a square.');
 }
}
void main() {
 var shapes = [Circle(), Square()];
 for (var shape in shapes) {
```

```dart
shape.draw(); // Polymorphic method call

  }

}
```

```
DartPad  <>   New    C Reset  ☰ Format   ↓  Install      poetic-aqueduct-2080  local edits        Samples ∨
              Pad                           SDK
1 ▾ class Shape {                              ► Run      Console
2 ▾  void draw() {
3     print('Drawing a shape.');                           Drawing a circle.
4    }                                                      Drawing a square.
5  }
6 ▾ class Circle extends Shape {
7    @override
8 ▾  void draw() {
9     print('Drawing a circle.');
10   }
11 }
12 ▾ class Square extends Shape {
13   @override
14 ▾  void draw() {
15    print('Drawing a square.');
16   }
17 }
18 ▾ void main() {
19   var shapes = [Circle(), Square()];
20 ▾ for (var shape in shapes) {
21    shape.draw(); // Polymorphic method call
22   }                                          Documentation
23 }
24                                              abstract class Flyable
```

In this example, we have a `Shape` class and two subclasses, `Circle` and `Square`. Each subclass overrides the `draw()` method with its own specific implementation. In the `main()` function, we create a list of shapes that contains instances of both `Circle` and `Square`. By invoking the `draw()` method on each object in the list, we achieve polymorphism. The appropriate `draw()` method implementation is dynamically determined at runtime based on the actual object type.

6.3.2 POLYMORPHISM WITH INTERFACES:

```dart
abstract class Animal {
  void makeSound();
}
class Dog implements Animal {
  @override
  void makeSound() {
    print('The dog barks.');
  }
}
class Cat implements Animal {
  @override
  void makeSound() {
    print('The cat meows.');
  }
}
void main() {
  var animals = [Dog(), Cat()];
  for (var animal in animals) {
    animal.makeSound(); // Polymorphic method call
  }
}
```

```dart
abstract class Animal {
  void makeSound();
}
class Dog implements Animal {
  @override
  void makeSound() {
  print('The dog barks.');
  }
}
class Cat implements Animal {
  @override
  void makeSound() {
  print('The cat meows.');
  }
}
void main() {
  var animals = [Dog(), Cat()];
for (var animal in animals) {
  animal.makeSound(); // Polymorphic method call
  }
}
```

Console

The dog barks.
The cat meows.

Documentation

class Shape

In this example, we define an `Animal` interface with a `makeSound()` method. The `Dog` and `Cat` classes implement the `Animal` interface and provide their own implementations of the `makeSound()` method. In the `main()` function, we create a list of animals that contains instances of both `Dog` and `Cat`. By invoking the `makeSound()` method on each object in the list, we achieve polymorphism. Each object responds to the method call with its specific implementation.

Polymorphism allows us to write code that can work with objects of different classes, if they adhere to a common superclass or interface. This flexibility enables us to create modular and extensible code, as new classes can be added without requiring changes to the existing codebase. Polymorphism enhances code reusability, promotes code abstraction, and makes the code more flexible and adaptable to different scenarios.

7 ERROR HANDLING AND EXCEPTION HANDLING

- Understanding errors and exceptions in Dart

  - Handling exceptions using try-catch blocks

  - Throwing and catching custom exceptions

  - Utilizing the `on` and `catch` clauses for specific exception handling

  - Examples illustrating error and exception handling in different scenarios

Error handling and exception handling are important aspects of writing robust and reliable code. Dart provides mechanisms to handle errors and exceptions using try-catch blocks and other related constructs. Here's an example of error handling and exception handling in DartPad:

7.1 EXAMPLE 1: HANDLING EXCEPTIONS WITH TRY-CATCH

```dart
void main() {
try {
int result = 10 ~/ 0; // Performing division by zero
print('Result: $result'); // This line won't execute
} catch (e) {
print('An exception occurred: $e'); // Output: An exception occurred:
IntegerDivisionByZeroException
}
}
```

```
1  void main() {
2    try {
3      int result = 10 ~/ 0; // Performing division by zero
4      print('Result: $result'); // This line won't execute
5    } catch (e) {
6      print('An exception occurred: \n $e'); // Output: An exception occu
7    }
8  }
9
```

Console

An exception occurred:
    Unsupported operation: Result of truncatin

In this example, we attempt to perform an integer division by zero, which would normally throw an `IntegerDivisionByZeroException`. To handle this exception, we enclose the potentially problematic code within a try block. If an exception occurs within the try block, the catch block is executed, and the exception is caught in the variable `e`. In the catch block, we print a custom error message along with the exception information.

7.2   EXAMPLE 2: HANDLING SPECIFIC EXCEPTIONS

```
void main() {
  try {
    int result = 10 ~/ 0; // Performing division by zero
    print('Result: $result'); // This line won't execute
  } on UnspportedError {
    print('Cannot divide by zero.'); // Output: Cannot divide by zero.
  }
}
```

```dart
void main() {
  try {
    int result = 10 ~/ 0; // Performing division by zero
    print('Result: $result'); // This line won't execute
  } on UnsupportedError{
    print('Cannot divide by zero.'); // Output: Cannot divide by zero.
  }
}
```

Console

Cannot divide by zero.

In this example, we use the `on` keyword to specify the specific exception type (`UnsupportedError`) that we want to handle. If this specific exception occurs within the try block, the corresponding catch block is executed. In this case, we print a custom error message indicating that division by zero is not possible.

Null safety in Dart is enforced to prevent errors caused by unintentional access to null variables. By utilizing sound null safety features, potential runtime errors are transformed into edit-time analysis errors, allowing developers to catch and address these errors before deploying their apps.

Dart considers all variables as non-nullable by default, meaning they are required to have a value. If a method expects a non-null value but receives null instead, it can lead to a runtime error known as a null dereference error. To specify that a variable can hold a null value, you can add a `?` after the type annotation, like `int? i`.

Dart provides several features to work with null values effectively:

8.1   LATE VARIABLES:

The `late` keyword allows declaring non-nullable variables without initializing them immediately. They can be assigned a value before accessing, but accessing them before assigning a value will result in a runtime error. Non-null Assertion Operator (`!`): When you are confident that a nullable variable will have a non-null value at a certain point, you can use the `!` operator to access it without null checks. However, if the variable is null at runtime, a runtime error will occur.

```
String? nullableString = 'ChatGPT';
String nonNullString = nullableString!;


print(nonNullString); // Outputs: ChatGPT
```

8.2 NULL AWARE OPERATORS

Dart includes null-aware operators to simplify working with nullable values. The `?.` operator allows accessing properties or methods on an object if it is not null, otherwise it returns null. The `..?` operator enables calling a sequence of methods on an object if it is not null.

```dart
class Person {
  String name;

  Person(this.name);
  void sayHello() {
    print('Hello, $name!');
  }
}
Person? person = Person('John');
person?.sayHello(); // Outputs: Hello, John!
person = null;
person?.sayHello(); // No output, as person is null
```

In this example, the nullableString variable is declared as nullable (String?). The non-null assertion operator (!) is used to assert that the value will not be null. The value of nullableString is assigned to nonNullString, which is a non-nullable String. When nonNullString is printed, it successfully outputs the assigned value.

8.3 LATE INITIALIZATION AND NULL SAFETY FOR FIELDS:

Dart allows marking instance fields as `late` or `late final`, allowing them to be initialized before being accessed, even if they cannot be assigned a value during construction.

```dart
class Example {
  late String lateField;
  late final String lateFinalField;

  Example() {
    lateField = 'Initialized late';
    lateFinalField = 'Initialized late final';
  }
}

void main() {
  var example = Example();

  print(example.lateField); // Outputs: Initialized late
  print(example.lateFinalField); // Outputs: Initialized late final
}
```

In this example, the Example class has two late-initialized fields: lateField and lateFinalField. They are declared using the late and late final keywords, respectively. The fields are initialized in the class's constructor before being accessed in the main function. The assigned values are successfully printed.

By leveraging these null safety features, developers can catch potential null reference errors at compile-time, leading to more robust and reliable code. It encourages better coding practices and reduces the likelihood of encountering null-related bugs during runtime.

While the non-null assertion operator (`!`) can be useful in certain cases, it should be used cautiously since incorrectly asserting a nullable expression as non-null can lead to runtime errors. Dart's null-aware operators and other null safety features are recommended for handling nullable values in a safer and more predictable manner.

9 EXERCISES WITH SOLUTIONS

9.1 EXERCISES

EXERCISE 1: CALCULATE TOTAL PRICE

Write a Dart function that takes in a list of prices for items in a shopping cart and calculates the total price. Then, test your function with a sample list of prices.

EXERCISE 2: APPLY DISCOUNT

Write a Dart function that takes in the original price of an item and a discount percentage and calculates the discounted price. Then, test your function with a sample original price and discount percentage.

EXERCISE 3: FIND EXPENSIVE ITEMS

Write a Dart function that takes in a list of item prices and a maximum price and returns a list of items that are more expensive than the maximum price. Then, test your function with a sample list of item prices and a maximum price.

EXERCISE 4: CALCULATE AVERAGE PRICE

Write a Dart function that takes in a list of prices for items in a shopping cart and calculates the average price. Then, test your function with a sample list of prices.

EXERCISE 5: APPLY TAX

Write a Dart function that takes in the original price of an item and a tax rate and calculates the final price including tax. Then, test your function with a sample original price and tax rate.

EXERCISE 6: FIND AFFORDABLE ITEMS

Write a Dart function that takes in a list of item prices and a maximum price and returns a list of items that are affordable (less than or equal to) the maximum price. Then, test your function with a sample list of item prices and a maximum price.

EXERCISE 7: SHOPPING CART WITH DISCOUNTED TOTAL

Create a shopping cart program that allows users to add items along with their prices to a cart. Implement a discount feature where if the total price exceeds a certain threshold, a discount is applied. Display the original total, discount amount, and final total. Prompt the user for input to add items and their prices.

EXERCISE 8: PRODUCT INVENTORY MANAGEMENT

Build a program that manages a product inventory. Implement functions to add new products, update quantities, and remove products from the inventory. Provide options for searching products by name or category. Allow the user to perform various operations on the inventory, such as checking stock levels and calculating the total value of the inventory.

EXERCISE 9: ONLINE ORDER FULFILLMENT

Design a system for processing online orders. Create classes for orders, customers, and products. Implement functions to add new orders, calculate order totals, and track order status. Provide options to search for orders by customer or product. Implement error handling for out-of-stock products or invalid order details.

EXERCISE 10: SALES REPORT GENERATOR

Build a program that generates sales reports based on a given dataset. Read data from a file or use a predefined list of sales records. Calculate and display various statistics, such as total sales, average sales per day, top-selling products, and sales by category. Allow the user to specify the time range for generating the report.

These exercises require a deeper understanding of Dart programming concepts and may involve concepts such as classes, file handling, data manipulation, and more.

9.2 CORRECTION

9.2.1 EXERCISE 1: CALCULATE TOTAL PRICE

```dart
void main() {
 List<double> prices = [10.99, 5.99, 8.99, 3.49];
double calculateTotalPrice(List<double> prices) {
 double total = 0;
 for (double price in prices) {
total += price;
 }
 return total;
 }
double totalPrice = calculateTotalPrice(prices);
 print('Total price: \$$totalPrice');
 }
```

The code correctly defines a function `calculateTotalPrice` that takes in a list of prices and calculates the total price by iterating through the list and adding up the prices. The function is then called with the `prices` list, and the calculated total price is printed.

9.2.2 EXERCISE 2: APPLY DISCOUNT

```dart
void main() {
 double applyDiscount(double originalPrice, double discountPercentage) {
 double discountAmount = originalPrice * (discountPercentage / 100);
 double discountedPrice = originalPrice - discountAmount;
 return discountedPrice;
 }
double originalPrice = 100.0;
 double discountPercentage = 20.0;
 double discountedPrice = applyDiscount(originalPrice, discountPercentage);
 print('Discounted price: \$$discountedPrice');
}
```

```
DartPad  <>   New Pad   C Reset  ☰ Format  ⬇ Install SDK      poetic-aqueduct-2080  [local edits]                Samples ⌄

1  void main() {                                                  ▶ Run      Console
2    double applyDiscount(double originalPrice, double discountPercentage)
3      double discountAmount = originalPrice * (discountPercentage / 100);      Discounted price: $80
4      double discountedPrice = originalPrice - discountAmount;
5      return discountedPrice;
6    }
7    double originalPrice = 100.0;
8    double discountPercentage = 20.0;
9    double discountedPrice = applyDiscount(originalPrice, discountPercenta
10   print('Discounted price: \$$discountedPrice');
11  }
12
```

The code defines a function `applyDiscount` that takes in the original price and discount percentage. It calculates the discount amount by multiplying the original price with the discount percentage divided by 100. Then, it subtracts the discount amount from the original price to get the discounted price. The function is called with the `originalPrice` and `discountPercentage`, and the resulting discounted price is printed.

9.2.3 EXERCISE 3: FIND EXPENSIVE ITEMS

```
void main() {
  List<double> itemPrices = [19.99, 9.99, 24.99, 14.99];
  double maxPrice = 15.0;
  List<double> findExpensiveItems(List<double> itemPrices, double maxPrice) {
    List<double> expensiveItems = [];
    for (double price in itemPrices) {
      if (price > maxPrice) {
        expensiveItems.add(price);
      }
    }
    return expensiveItems;
  }
  List<double> expensiveItems = findExpensiveItems(itemPrices, maxPrice);
  print('Expensive items: $expensiveItems');
}
```

```
1 ▾ void main() {
2    List<double> itemPrices = [19.99, 9.99, 24.99, 14.99];
3    double maxPrice = 15.0;
4 ▾ List<double> findExpensiveItems(List<double> itemPrices, double maxPric
5    List<double> expensiveItems = [];
6 ▾  for (double price in itemPrices) {
7 ▾   if (price > maxPrice) {
8       expensiveItems.add(price);
9      }
10   }
11    return expensiveItems;
12   }
13   List<double> expensiveItems = findExpensiveItems(itemPrices, maxPrice);
14    print('Expensive items: $expensiveItems');
15  }
16
```

Console

Expensive items: [19.99, 24.99]

The code defines a function `findExpensiveItems` that takes in a list of item prices and a maximum price. It iterates through the `itemPrices` list and checks if each price is greater than the `maxPrice`. If a price is greater, it adds it to the `expensiveItems` list. Finally, the function returns the `expensiveItems` list. The function is called with the `itemPrices` and `maxPrice`, and the resulting list of expensive items is printed.

You can copy the codes and run or modify them in DartPad to see the output and further explore and modify the code as per your learning goals

9.2.4 EXERCISE 4: CALCULATE AVERAGE PRICE

```dart
void main() {
 List<double> prices = [10.99, 5.99, 8.99, 3.49];
 double calculateAveragePrice(List<double> prices) {
 double sum = 0;
 for (double price in prices) {
 sum += price;
 }
```

```
return sum / prices.length;
}
double averagePrice = calculateAveragePrice(prices);
print('Average price: \$$averagePrice');
}
```

```
1 ▼  void main() {                                              ► Run      Console
2      List<double> prices = [10.99, 5.99, 8.99, 3.49];
3 ▼  double calculateAveragePrice(List<double> prices) {                    Average price: $7.365
4      double sum = 0;
5 ▼    for (double price in prices) {
6      sum += price;
7      }
8      return sum / prices.length;
9      }
10   double averagePrice = calculateAveragePrice(prices);
11     print('Average price: \$$averagePrice');
12   }
13
```

The code defines a function `calculateAveragePrice` that takes in a list of prices and calculates the average price. It initializes a `sum` variable to 0 and then iterates through the `prices` list, adding each price to the sum. After the loop, it divides the sum by the length of the `prices` list to calculate the average price. The function is called with the `prices` list, and the resulting average price is printed.

9.2.5 EXERCISE 5: APPLY TAX

```
void main() {
 double applyTax(double originalPrice, double taxRate) {
 double taxAmount = originalPrice * (taxRate / 100);
 double finalPrice = originalPrice + taxAmount;
```

```
    return finalPrice;
  }

double originalPrice = 100.0;

double taxRate = 7.5;

double finalPrice = applyTax(originalPrice, taxRate);

print('Final price including tax: \$$finalPrice');

}
```

The code defines a function `applyTax` that takes in the original price and tax rate. It calculates the tax amount by multiplying the original price with the tax rate divided by 100. Then, it adds the tax amount to the original price to get the final price including tax. The function is called with the `originalPrice` and `taxRate`, and the resulting final price is printed.

9.2.6 EXERCISE 6: FIND AFFORDABLE ITEMS

```dart
void main() {
  List<double> itemPrices = [19.99, 9.99, 24.99, 14.99];
  double maxPrice = 15.0;
List<double> findAffordableItems(List<double> itemPrices, double maxPrice) {
  List<double> affordableItems = [];
  for (double price in itemPrices) {
  if (price <= maxPrice) {
  affordableItems.add(price);
  }
  }
  return affordableItems;
  }
  List<double> affordableItems = findAffordableItems(itemPrices, maxPrice);
  print('Affordable items: $affordableItems');
}
```

The code defines a function `findAffordableItems` that takes in a list of item prices and a maximum price. It iterates through the `itemPrices` list and checks if each price is less than or equal to the `maxPrice`. If a price is affordable, it adds it to the `affordableItems` list. Finally, the function returns the `affordableItems` list. The function is called with the `itemPrices` and `maxPrice`, and the resulting list of affordable items is printed.

9.2.7 EXERCISE 7: SHOPPING CART WITH DISCOUNTED TOTAL:

1. Create a class for the shopping cart and define properties such as items (a list to store the items) and total (to keep track of the total price).

2. Implement methods to add items to the cart, calculate the total price, and apply any discounts based on certain conditions.

3. Prompt the user for input to add items and their prices. Store them in the cart and update the total accordingly.

4. Define rules for applying discounts, such as a minimum threshold for the total price, and implement the discount calculation logic accordingly.

5. Display the original total, discount amount, and final total to the user.

Here is an example code implementation for this Exercise:

```
class ShoppingCart {
List<double> items = [];
double total = 0;
```

```
void addItem(double price) {
  items.add(price);
  total += price;
}
void applyDiscount(double threshold, double discountPercentage) {
  if (total > threshold) {
  double discountAmount = total * (discountPercentage / 100);
  total -= discountAmount;
  }
}
void displayTotal() {
  print('Original Total: \$${total.toStringAsFixed(2)}');
}
}
void main() {
  ShoppingCart cart = ShoppingCart();
  // Adding items to the cart
  cart.addItem(10.99);
  cart.addItem(5.99);
  cart.addItem(8.99);
  cart.addItem(3.49);
  // Applying discount if the total exceeds $30 with a 10% discount
  cart.applyDiscount(30.0, 10.0);
  // Displaying the final total
```

```
    cart.displayTotal();

}
```

```dart
class ShoppingCart {
  List<double> items = [];
  double total = 0;
  void addItem(double price) {
    items.add(price);
    total += price;
  }
  void applyDiscount(double threshold, double discountPercentage) {
    if (total > threshold) {
      double discountAmount = total * (discountPercentage / 100);
      total -= discountAmount;
    }
  }
  void displayTotal() {
    print('Original Total: \$${total.toStringAsFixed(2)}');
  }
}
void main() {
  ShoppingCart cart = ShoppingCart();
  // Adding items to the cart
  cart.addItem(10.99);
  cart.addItem(5.99);
  cart.addItem(8.99);
  cart.addItem(3.49);
  // Applying discount if the total exceeds $30 with a 10% discount
  cart.applyDiscount(30.0, 10.0);
  // Displaying the final total
  cart.displayTotal();
}
```

Console

Original Total: $29.46

In the code above, we define a class `ShoppingCart` that represents the shopping cart. It has properties `items` (a list to store the item prices) and `total` (to keep track of the total price).

The class provides methods to `addItem` which adds an item to the cart and updates the total price, `applyDiscount` which applies a discount if the total price exceeds a certain threshold, and `displayTotal` which displays the original total.

In the `main` function, we create an instance of the `ShoppingCart` class and add some items to the cart using the `addItem` method. Then, we apply a discount if the total price exceeds $30 with a 10% discount using the `applyDiscount` method. Finally, we display the original total using the `displayTotal` method.

When you run this code, it will calculate the original total of the items in the cart and apply the discount if applicable, displaying the final total to the console.

9.2.8 EXERCISE 8: PRODUCT INVENTORY MANAGEMENT

Here is a high-level overview of the steps you can follow:

1. Create a class for the product, defining properties such as name, category, and quantity.

2. Implement functions to add new products, update quantities, and remove products from the inventory. You can use a list or a map to store the products.

3. Provide options for searching products by name or category. Implement search functions accordingly.

4. Allow the user to perform various operations on the inventory, such as checking stock levels and calculating the total value of the inventory. Implement functions for these operations.

Here's an example code implementation for Exercise: Product Inventory Management :

```
class Product {
String name;
String category;
int quantity;
Product(this.name, this.category, this.quantity);
}
class Inventory {
```

```dart
List<Product> products = [];
void addProduct(String name, String category, int quantity) {
Product newProduct = Product(name, category, quantity);
products.add(newProduct);
print('Product added: $name');
}
void updateQuantity(String name, int quantity) {
Product? product = findProductByName(name);
if (product != null) {
product.quantity = quantity;
print('Quantity updated: $name');
} else {
print('Product not found: $name');
}
}

void removeProduct(String name) {
Product? product = findProductByName(name);
if (product != null) {
products.remove(product);
print('Product removed: $name');
} else {
print('Product not found: $name');
}
}
void displayStockLevels() {
```

```dart
  for (Product product in products) {
    print('${product.name} - Quantity: ${product.quantity}');
  }
}

Product? findProductByName(String name) {
  for (Product product in products) {
    if (product.name == name) {
      return product;
    }
  }
  return null;
}

void main() {
  Inventory inventory = Inventory();
  // Adding products to the inventory
  inventory.addProduct('Apple', 'Fruits', 10);
  inventory.addProduct('Banana', 'Fruits', 15);
  inventory.addProduct('Carrot', 'Vegetables', 20);
  // Updating quantity of a product
  inventory.updateQuantity('Apple', 5);
  // Removing a product from the inventory
  inventory.removeProduct('Banana');
  // Displaying stock levels
```

```
    inventory.displayStockLevels();
}
```

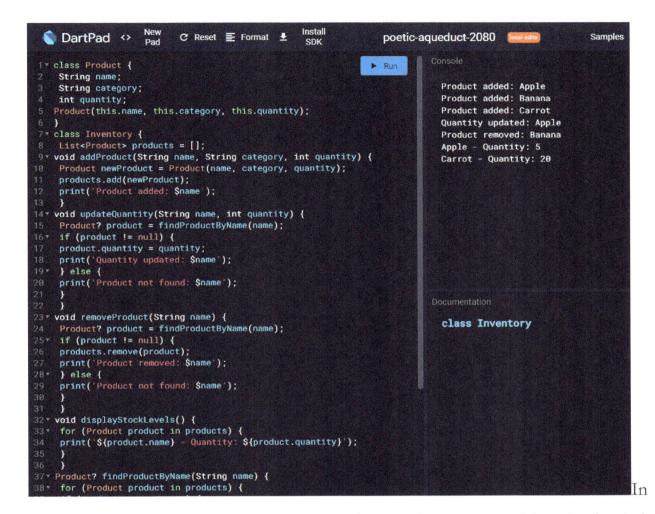

```
1 ▼ class Product {
2      String name;
3      String category;
4      int quantity;
5      Product(this.name, this.category, this.quantity);
6   }
7 ▼ class Inventory {
8      List<Product> products = [];
9 ▼   void addProduct(String name, String category, int quantity) {
10       Product newProduct = Product(name, category, quantity);
11       products.add(newProduct);
12       print('Product added: $name');
13     }
14 ▼   void updateQuantity(String name, int quantity) {
15       Product? product = findProductByName(name);
16 ▼     if (product != null) {
17         product.quantity = quantity;
18         print('Quantity updated: $name');
19 ▼     } else {
20         print('Product not found: $name');
21       }
22     }
23 ▼   void removeProduct(String name) {
24       Product? product = findProductByName(name);
25 ▼     if (product != null) {
26         products.remove(product);
27         print('Product removed: $name');
28 ▼     } else {
29         print('Product not found: $name');
30       }
31     }
32 ▼   void displayStockLevels() {
33       for (Product product in products) {
34         print('${product.name} - Quantity: ${product.quantity}');
35       }
36     }
37 ▼   Product? findProductByName(String name) {
38 ▼     for (Product product in products) {
```

Console

```
Product added: Apple
Product added: Banana
Product added: Carrot
Quantity updated: Apple
Product removed: Banana
Apple - Quantity: 5
Carrot - Quantity: 20
```

Documentation

class Inventory

In the code above, we define two classes: `Product` and `Inventory`. The `Product` class represents a product with properties like `name`, `category`, and `quantity`. The `Inventory` class represents the product inventory and has a list of `Product` objects.

The `Inventory` class provides methods to `addProduct` which adds a new product to the inventory, `updateQuantity` which updates the quantity of a product by searching for it by name, `removeProduct` which removes a product from the inventory by name, and `displayStockLevels` which displays the stock levels of all the products in the inventory.

In the `main` function, we create an instance of the `Inventory` class and add some products to the inventory using the `addProduct` method. Then, we update the quantity of a product using the `updateQuantity` method and remove a product using the `removeProduct` method. Finally, we display the stock levels of all the products using the `displayStockLevels` method.

When you run this code, it will perform the operations on the inventory, such as adding, updating, and removing products, and display the stock levels of all the products in the inventory.

9.2.9 EXERCISE 9: ONLINE ORDER FULFILLMENT

Here is a general outline:

1. Create classes for orders, customers, and products, defining relevant properties for each.

2. Implement functions to add new orders, calculate order totals, and track order status. Store the orders, customers, and products in appropriate data structures such as lists or maps.

3. Provide options to search for orders by customer or product. Implement search functions accordingly.

4. Implement error handling for out-of-stock products or invalid order details, such as checking if the requested quantity is available in the inventory.

Here's an example code implementation for Exercise: Online Order Fulfillment:

```
class Product {
String name;
double price;
```

```dart
  int quantity;
  Product(this.name, this.price, this.quantity);
}
class Customer {
  String name;
  String address;
  Customer(this.name, this.address);
}
class Order {
  Customer customer;
  List<Product> products;
  bool isFulfilled;
  Order(this.customer, this.products) : isFulfilled = false;
  double calculateTotal() {
    double total = 0;
    for (Product product in products) {
      total += product.price * product.quantity;
    }
    return total;
  }
}
class OrderManager {
  List<Order> orders = [];
  void addOrder(Customer customer, List<Product> products) {
    Order newOrder = Order(customer, products);
```

```dart
    orders.add(newOrder);

    print('Order added for ${customer.name}');

    }

void fulfillOrder(Order order) {

    order.isFulfilled = true;

    print('Order fulfilled for ${order.customer.name}');

    }

List<Order> findOrdersByCustomer(String customerName) {

    List<Order> matchingOrders = [];

    for (Order order in orders) {

    if (order.customer.name == customerName) {

    matchingOrders.add(order);

    }

    }

    return matchingOrders;

    }

List<Order> findOrdersByProduct(String productName) {

    List<Order> matchingOrders = [];

    for (Order order in orders) {

    for (Product product in order.products) {

    if (product.name == productName) {

    matchingOrders.add(order);

    break;

    }

    }
```

```dart
  }
  return matchingOrders;
  }
}
void main() {
 Product product1 = Product('Phone', 799.99, 1);
 Product product2 = Product('Laptop', 1299.99, 2);
 Product product3 = Product('Headphones', 149.99, 3);
Customer customer1 = Customer('Omar Hanafi', 'Skhirat');
 Customer customer2 = Customer('Imane Malik', 'Said Hajji');
OrderManager orderManager = OrderManager();
// Add orders
 orderManager.addOrder(customer1, [product1, product2]);
 orderManager.addOrder(customer2, [product3]);
// Fulfill an order
List<Order> customer1Orders = orderManager.findOrdersByCustomer('Omar
Hanafi');
 if (customer1Orders.isNotEmpty) {
 Order order = customer1Orders[0];
 orderManager.fulfillOrder(order);
 }
// Find orders by product
List<Order> product1Orders = orderManager.findOrdersByProduct('Phone');
 if (product1Orders.isNotEmpty) {
 print('Orders containing Phone:');
```

```
for (Order order in product1Orders) {

print(order.customer.name);

}

}

}
```

```
43     return matchingOrders;
44   }
45 ▾ List<Order> findOrdersByProduct(String productName) {
46     List<Order> matchingOrders = [];
47 ▾ for (Order order in orders) {
48 ▾ for (Product product in order.products) {
49 ▾ if (product.name == productName) {
50     matchingOrders.add(order);
51     break;
52   }
53   }
54   }
55     return matchingOrders;
56   }
57 }
58 ▾ void main() {
59     Product product1 = Product('Phone', 799.99, 1);
60     Product product2 = Product('Laptop', 1299.99, 2);
61     Product product3 = Product('Headphones', 149.99, 3);
62   Customer customer1 = Customer('Omar Hanafi', 'Skhirat');
63     Customer customer2 = Customer('Imane Malik', 'Said Hajji');
64   OrderManager orderManager = OrderManager();
65   // Add orders
66     orderManager.addOrder(customer1, [product1, product2]);
67     orderManager.addOrder(customer2, [product3]);
68   // Fulfill an order
69     List<Order> customer1Orders = orderManager.findOrdersByCustomer('Omar
70 ▾ if (customer1Orders.isNotEmpty) {
71     Order order = customer1Orders[0];
72     orderManager.fulfillOrder(order);
73   }
74   // Find orders by product
75     List<Order> product1Orders = orderManager.findOrdersByProduct('Phone'
76 ▾ if (product1Orders.isNotEmpty) {
77     print('Orders containing Phone:');
78 ▾ for (Order order in product1Orders) {
79     print(order.customer.name);
80   }
```

Console

```
Order added for Omar Hanafi
Order added for Imane Malik
Order fulfilled for Omar Hanafi
Orders containing Phone:
Omar Hanafi
```

In the code above, we define three classes: `Product`, `Customer`, and `Order`. The `Product` class represents a product with properties like `name`, `price`, and `quantity`. The `Customer` class represents a customer with properties like `name` and `address`. The `Order` class represents an order with properties like `customer`, `products`, and `isFulfilled`.

The `Order` class provides a method `calculateTotal` which calculates the total cost of the order based on the price and quantity of the products.

The `OrderManager` class is responsible for managing the orders. It has a list of orders and provides methods like `addOrder` to add a new order, `fulfillOrder` to mark an order as fulfilled, and `findOrdersByCustomer` and `findOrdersByProduct` to search for orders based on customer or product.

In the `main` function, we create instances of `Product`, `Customer`, and `OrderManager`. We add some orders using the `addOrder` method, fulfill an order using the `fulfillOrder` method, and find orders by customer and product using the `findOrdersByCustomer` and `findOrdersByProduct` methods.

When you run this code, it will perform the operations on the orders, such as adding orders, fulfilling orders, and finding orders based on customer or product.

9.2.10   EXERCISE 10: SALES REPORT GENERATOR

Here is an outline for this exercise:

1. Read the sales data from a file or use a predefined list of sales records.

2. Parse the data and store it in appropriate data structures.

3. Implement functions to calculate and display various statistics, such as total sales, average sales per day, top-selling products, and sales by category.

4. Allow the user to specify the time range for generating the report and filter the data accordingly.

```dart
class Sale {
  String product;
  double price;
  DateTime date;
  Sale(this.product, this.price, this.date);
}
class SalesReportGenerator {
  List<Sale> sales;
  SalesReportGenerator(this.sales);
  void generateReport(DateTime startDate, DateTime endDate) {
    List<Sale> filteredSales = sales
      .where((sale) => sale.date.isAfter(startDate) && sale.date.isBefore(endDate))
      .toList();
    double totalSales = 0;
    for (Sale sale in filteredSales) {
      totalSales += sale.price;
    }
    print('Sales Report');
    print('Start Date: $startDate');
    print('End Date: $endDate');
    print('Total Sales: \$${totalSales.toStringAsFixed(2)}');
    print('Number of Sales: ${filteredSales.length}');
    // Additional statistics or formatting can be added as per requirements
  }
```

```dart
}
void main() {
// Sample sales data
List<Sale> sales = [
Sale('Product 1', 10.99, DateTime(2023, 6, 1)),
Sale('Product 2', 15.99, DateTime(2023, 6, 2)),
Sale('Product 3', 20.99, DateTime(2023, 6, 3)),
Sale('Product 4', 5.99, DateTime(2023, 6, 4)),
Sale('Product 5', 12.99, DateTime(2023, 6, 5)),
];
SalesReportGenerator reportGenerator = SalesReportGenerator(sales);
// Generate report for a specific time range
DateTime startDate = DateTime(2023, 6, 1);
DateTime endDate = DateTime(2023, 6, 5);
reportGenerator.generateReport(startDate, endDate);
}
```

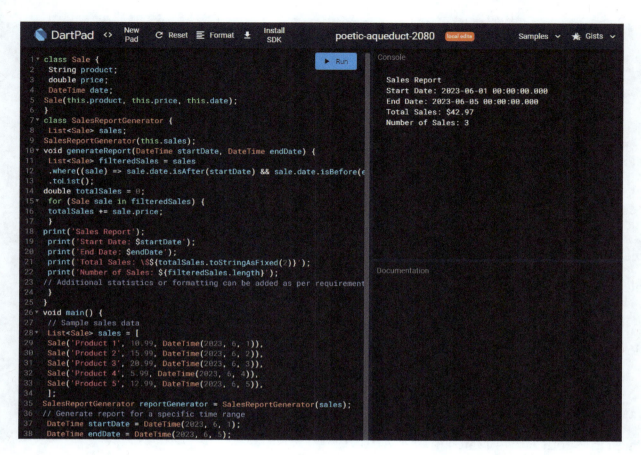

```dart
class Sale {
  String product;
  double price;
  DateTime date;
  Sale(this.product, this.price, this.date);
}
class SalesReportGenerator {
  List<Sale> sales;
  SalesReportGenerator(this.sales);
  void generateReport(DateTime startDate, DateTime endDate) {
    List<Sale> filteredSales = sales
    .where((sale) => sale.date.isAfter(startDate) && sale.date.isBefore(e
    .toList();
    double totalSales = 0;
    for (Sale sale in filteredSales) {
      totalSales += sale.price;
    }
    print('Sales Report');
    print('Start Date: $startDate');
    print('End Date: $endDate');
    print('Total Sales: \$${totalSales.toStringAsFixed(2)}');
    print('Number of Sales: ${filteredSales.length}');
    // Additional statistics or formatting can be added as per requirement
  }
}
void main() {
  // Sample sales data
  List<Sale> sales = [
    Sale('Product 1', 10.99, DateTime(2023, 6, 1)),
    Sale('Product 2', 15.99, DateTime(2023, 6, 2)),
    Sale('Product 3', 20.99, DateTime(2023, 6, 3)),
    Sale('Product 4', 5.99, DateTime(2023, 6, 4)),
    Sale('Product 5', 12.99, DateTime(2023, 6, 5)),
  ];
  SalesReportGenerator reportGenerator = SalesReportGenerator(sales);
  // Generate report for a specific time range
  DateTime startDate = DateTime(2023, 6, 1);
  DateTime endDate = DateTime(2023, 6, 5);
```

Console

```
Sales Report
Start Date: 2023-06-01 00:00:00.000
End Date: 2023-06-05 00:00:00.000
Total Sales: $42.97
Number of Sales: 3
```

Here is an example code implementation for Exercise: Sales Report Generator:

In the code above, we define a `Sale` class representing a sale with properties like `product`, `price`, and `date`. We also define a `SalesReportGenerator` class that takes a list of `Sale` objects in its constructor.

The `SalesReportGenerator` class provides a method called `generateReport` that takes a start date and an end date. It filters the sales based on the provided date range and calculates the total sales and the number of sales within that range. It then prints a sales report with the relevant information.

In the `main` function, we create a sample list of `Sale` objects and create an instance of the `SalesReportGenerator` class with the sales data. We then generate a report for a specific time range by providing the start and end dates to the `generateReport` method.

When you run this code, it will generate a sales report for the specified time range, displaying the total sales and the number of sales within that range.